GETTING MARRIED

From Courtship to Marriage

GERMÁN MARTÍNEZ

Liguori
ONE LIGUORI DRIVE
LIGUORI MO 63057-9999

Contents

Imprimi Potest: Thomas D. Picton, C.Ss.R., Provincial, Denver Province, The Redemptorists

Imprimatur: Most Reverend Robert J. Hermann, Auxiliary Bishop, Archdiocese of St. Louis

ISBN 978-0-7648-1638-3

Printed in the United States of America
07 08 09 10 11 5 4 3 2 1

Liguori Publications, a nonprofit corporation, is an apostolate of the Redemptorists. To learn more about the Redemptorists, visit **Redemptorists.com**.

To order, call 1-800-325-9521
www.liguori.org

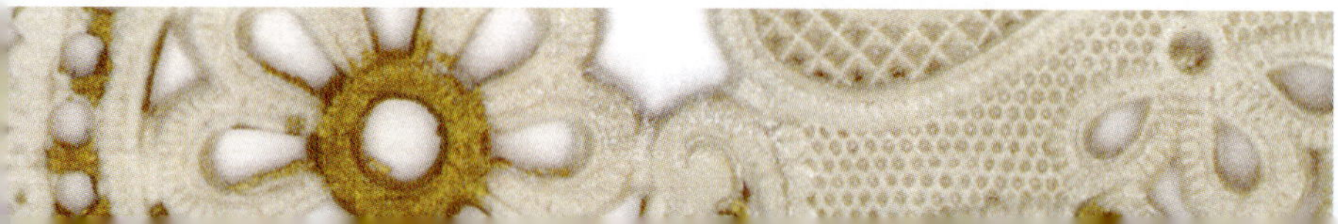

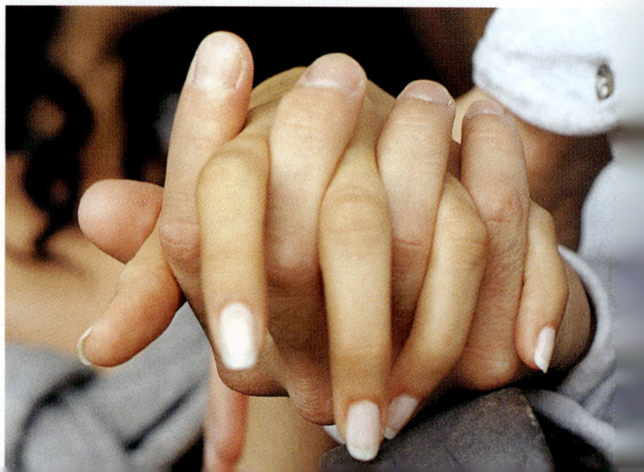

Introduction

Everyone is looking for happiness and love. Most of us experience them through the covenant of marriage. Young adults especially dream about experiencing this kind of love. However, they often misunderstand the true meaning of this bond and lack the attitudes and skills needed for successful relationships.

The material in this booklet has been drawn from the experiences of many married and engaged couples. It will help couples begin their journey from dating to married life and support them during their first years of marriage. The first section highlights the five pillars of choosing a partner and building a happy relationship. The second section highlights the five facets of a lifelong, holy marriage. As each relationship is unique, you must reflect upon these points in the context of your own circumstances.

VEER

You are preparing for a life journey, not just a wedding. For a Christian couple, this requires a sincere turning to God's marvelous plan (Genesis 1:26–31) through the mystery of Christ. Your primary purpose as a couple is to invite Christ into your lives for, without him, you "can do nothing" (John 15:5). Both the natural and spiritual dimensions are fundamental to a graced-filled relationship. You can discover love and happiness and live them to the fullest by seeking God and following your heart. God created you and wants you to be happy, to love and be loved—the essence of life.

The Ideal Person

INDEXOPEN

Five Pillars for Marrying Well

Drew and Mary have been dating for a few years. They have developed a strong and intimate friendship, growing as a couple while remaining true to their Christian beliefs. They recently became engaged and are carefully planning their marriage and life together.

Rich and Julie met in college and fell in love. After graduation, they decided to move in together. For them, this arrangement was the best of both worlds. Rent was shared, and there was no need to permanently commit to each other; if they no longer felt love, they could leave. After a few years of living together, Rich decided the relationship seemed good enough and suggested they get married.

In your opinion, Which of the two engaged couples are more likely to have a successful marriage?

Decades of statistics are clear: Couples like Drew and Mary have a better chance of having a successful marriage. Even after a formal marriage, Rich and Julie face a greater chance of divorce. No one dates or marries to prepare for divorce, and no formula can predict the success or failure of the complex relationship that is marriage. People change and life events affect relationships in unpredictable ways. Nevertheless, many successful marriages are built on five pillars: physical attraction, genuine friendship, affective and effective independence, empathy and growth, and shared spirituality.

Physical Attraction. Most couples marry because of an initial physical attraction and the ultimate love that develops. However, finding a compatible person for a deep and meaningful relationship is more challenging than just "falling in love." The physical attraction people call "chemistry" should not be the decisive factor in determining whether a relationship will work. Though real and very often independent of our will, feelings perceived as love could ultimately be only lust, which is not a solid basis for a lasting relationship. A couple must strive to see a deeper compatibility, one that grows into a wholehearted commitment.

The ideal person doesn't exist. Since this may not be evident when lovers are alone and enclosed in their own cozy world, they should spend as much time as possible with friends and relatives to observe one another's interactions. These interactions in a variety of circumstances, especially when irritations and tensions arise, reveal a great deal about personality. For example, a woman can learn a lot about her fiancé when she observes his willingness to help clear the table after a family dinner. The small, seemingly unimportant behaviors and actions, or lack thereof, often tell the most about someone's personality.

Genuine Friendship. True romance develops out of friendship and trust. Like physical attraction, friendship is only one element of marital success, but friendship infuses all other aspects of the relationship with meaning. To be "best friends" indicates a kind of compatibility far deeper than the infatuation between lovers. The former—I need you because I love you—can lead to a warm and rewarding relationship, opening hearts so the couple can share their lives together. The latter—I love you because I need you—reflects immaturity. Loyal and loving friends are not judgmental, nor do they stifle individual energies. They support and cherish the other as he or she is.

It is important to note that the happiness a couple experiences during their engagement does not guarantee a successful marriage. A couple should approach marriage understanding that things will not always run smoothly. A husband and wife are called to be soul mates, knowing their mutual intimate desires and supporting each other's aspirations despite the challenges that might arise. Let *divine* friendship be at the center of *your* friendship, so you may live your marital partnership to the fullest.

Affective and Effective Independence. A real ability to fulfill each other's needs, both emotional and physical, is required to create an intimate life of love. If the couple's personal lives are to grow and mature, they must depend on one another and be independent from outside interference. A secure spouse does not depend too much on his or her parents or friends for emotional support. Your loyalty is to your partner, and that relationship comes first. This independence and interdependence should not stifle each other, however, because individual space and outside interests enrich the relationship.

Second, effective independence is demonstrated in financial matters. You must budget money for monthly bills: housing, food, insurance, and so forth. This budget should also include money for personal interests and goals such as further education or hobbies. Economic issues cause most of the difficulties couples face, especially during the first years of marriage. The more a couple is a good team in financial planning, the better they will be able to find their way through tough times.

Empathy and Growth. Getting to know one another is the fruit of honest dialogue and sincere communication. Thus, it is essential to talk frequently about important decisions and goals before committing yourselves to marriage. If these discussions do not deepen your relationship, you may not know *yourself* and may be unable or unwilling to let someone else know you. Dating with a purpose leads to personal growth through *empathy*, the capacity for sharing feelings and ideas through friendship and communication. Effective communication involves more than mere words. It is not only sharing information; it is sharing yourself by opening your heart.

Knowing your partner depends a great deal on listening and understanding his or her values and beliefs on topics such as marital roles, individual expectations, sexual love, parenting, finances, work and leisure times, relationship with families and friends, and social life. A strong couple is able to accept differences in personality and resolve conflicts.

You should not go into marriage intending to change your partner. Marriage itself does not change a person, though you can pray to the Holy Spirit for a change in a specific situation.

Shared Spirituality. Our hunger for human love points us to the ultimate love, our love of God, the only and complete fulfillment of our lives. As couples search for love, they are really seeking God. Thus, it is the spouse's duty to help his or her partner grow spiritually. A living faith enables a couple to transform their love from "I and you" to "we," for they see themselves as God's gift to each other. The couple encounters God in a real and tangible way—their relationship. Saint Paul speaks of love as the higher gift: "Love is patient; love is kind...Love never ends" (1 Corinthians 13:4–8). Scripture begins (Genesis) and ends (Revelation) with God's love mirrored in the spousal image. Song of Solomon 3:1–4 also displays the beauty of this love:

> *Upon my bed at night I sought him whom my soul loves;*
> *I sought him, but found him not; I called him, but he gave no answer. "I will rise now and go about the city, in the streets and in the squares; I will seek him whom my soul loves."*
> *I sought him, but found him not. The sentinels found me, as they went about in the city. "Have you seen him whom my soul loves?" Scarcely had I passed them, when I found him whom my soul loves. I held him, and would not let him go.*

Marital happiness and fulfillment depend largely on sharing healthy values. Sharing a common faith and a personal relationship with God through prayer and the sacraments, both individually and as a couple, is essential for a Christian. Married life, like faith, is multifaceted and cannot be reduced to a set of rules or ideals. Couples who center their lives on a personal relationship with Christ and on the Eucharist, however, find their relationship is solid.

Engaged! How to Grow in Lasting Love

DYNAMIC GRAPHICS

Mike and Kelly had been seeing each other for about two years when the subject of marriage came up. At first, romantic feelings and expressions had defined their relationship. With the passage of time, though, their relationship and their conversations evolved. Like good friends, they shared differences and disappointments along with joys and appreciation.

Once Mike and Kelly started talking about marriage, they couldn't stop! Nearly every conversation turned to their expectations and dreams of married life. One night while visiting close friends, Mike surprised Kelly with an engagement ring. As he held out the ring, Mike said simply: "I can't see my life without you." Kelly beamed and threw her arms around Mike as their friends cheered and congratulated them.

Do you remember when you first started talking about getting married?

Giving Yourself: The Key to Success

Many couples think marriage is like a business arrangement in which each person commits 50% to the relationship. But this approach is bound to fail. Why? Experience tells us that our intentions often miss the mark. Thus, if one intends to give 50% to the marriage commitment and depends on the other person to give an equal 50%, chances are the couple will never arrive at a 100% commitment. Marriage is a 100/100 proposition; not a 50/50 one.

When Does a Marriage Work?

A marriage will be successful if the couple understands that on their wedding day they must give themselves completely to each other. When the couple forms a relationship of self-donation for life according to God's plan, they find personal fulfillment. Each partner has committed himself or herself to take care of the other completely and exclusively.

However, giving yourself does not solely consist of making a decision or fulfilling a desire; it also includes your emotional maturity and interpersonal skills. Be aware of the present and ever-changing needs and emotions of your partner; respond to them with love and support. For example, are you willing to listen to each other and seriously consider your partner's feelings?

Know yourself. It is important for each person in the relationship to know who he or she is, and where he or she came from. The family you grew up in tends to be the basis for your assumptions about other people's behavior and actions. This can sometimes lead to misunderstanding and conflict. For example, if your parents were not communicative or affectionate with each other, it may be hard for you to be a good communicator and lover. The person you are marrying also has a unique family history. Pay attention to serious unresolved issues in your families and address them. For example, "I haven't spoken to my mother in five years" is something you need to address. The virtues needed for a solid relationship are not innate; you must work to acquire them with God's assistance.

As you begin your life together as a couple, you will be gradually transformed—with God's grace. Ask yourself, What are my weaknesses and my virtues, and how will they affect our marriage? Will we allow God's grace grow and change us? Are we going to love each other unconditionally? How are we helping each other grow in holiness? Are we ready to assume our obligations as Christian parents and recognize our parental responsibilities? Do we pray together? Are we patient with one another? These are some basics of marital spirituality, virtues that have to be nurtured throughout your married life.

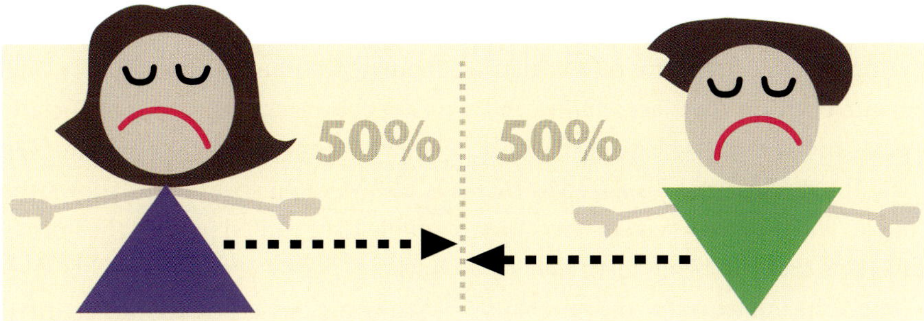

Love and Sex

The Catholic Church teaches that couples should abstain from having premarital relations and enter marriage in a state of God's grace. Premarital sex is never a good idea; it limits the couple's freedom as they approach marriage and promotes the physical aspect of sexual intimacy at the expense of the deeper qualities of the relationship. It also ignores the basic meaning of sexual intercourse and dampens romantic motivation in the crucial phase of preparation for a lifelong commitment. In addition, a couple who has had premarital sex feels a sense of "obligation" to each other—a false attachment. This obligation diminishes the couple's ability to freely understand, choose, and enter marriage. Only love founded on freedom can be the bedrock of a lasting marriage.

Sexuality is not a thing to be used to satisfy our wants. Sexuality is what we are, not what we give; it is the way God made us. Sexual love requires the whole person, not just the body, and it is meant to honor and serve your partner. Today's strange social "rules" of sexual behavior have shattered many dreams; they limit our freedom to love and be loved. Often one partner tells the other, "if you love me, you'll have sex with me." Wanting to please, the partner often consents. But the couple often loses respect for each other once they have satisfied their sexual desires. They become objects to satisfy each other's immediate physical needs, not emotionally and spiritually connected partners.

Respect and fidelity go hand-in-hand. When a man tells his girlfriend he loves her and wants to have sex with her, the best response she can give is "If you truly love me, let us have the courage to abstain from sex now and wait until we are married." This sacrifice is a great indicator of the boyfriend's true intentions and his willingness to respect his girlfriend's wishes.

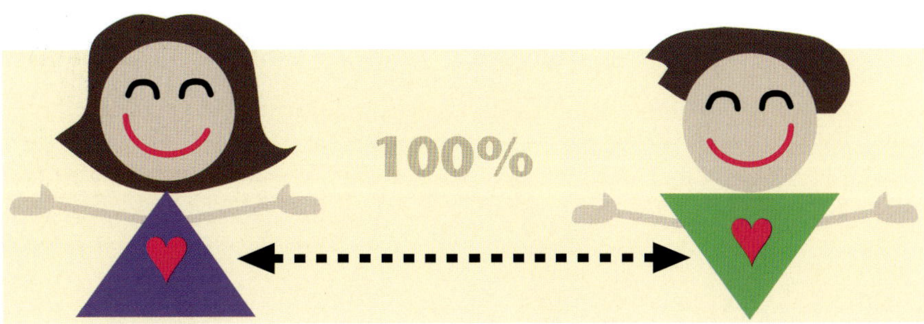

The Catholic Church speaks of the two inseparable functions of sexual intercourse within marriage: *unitive* and *procreative*. The *unitive* aspect refers to the intimate closeness displayed by the couple. The *procreative* aspect refers to a covenant that can bring forth life.

The Church insists on generous and responsible parenthood without contraceptives. As an alternative to artificial birth control, the Church proposes natural family planning (NFP), natural methods that monitor the woman's menstrual cycle to prevent or increase the chance of pregnancy. NFP is not contraception, which artificially blocks the means of creating life; NFP is always open to life and allows the couple to be united in both the unitive and procreative aspects of sexual love. Many parishes enlist trained married parishioners to inform engaged couples of these methods, and many hospitals also offer classes. For more information, contact your parish priest or the Couple to Couple League.

PHOTOS.COM

Couples who use NFP demonstrate affection and respect when they abstain from sexual intercourse during the woman's brief period of fertility. Thus, they are able to appreciate each other deeply as they exchange a variety of gestures of caring and love. Furthermore, the couple's intimacy can reach full culmination in their sexual union.

The physical communication of sexual union reveals that verbal language is only part of a relationship. Through the surrender of their bodies, couples are able to share the gift of self with each other. Intimate sharing can reveal the best of each partner: unselfish acceptance and commitment, affirmation of self-worth and sexual attraction, and an infinite amount of other blessings.

Although the joy of passionate love is felt in many ways, not all sexual expression is a romantic demonstration of love and respect. Perfect, pure sexuality does not exist. Couples should be aware of possible manipulations, past fears, and erroneous ideas about sex. Sexuality is beautiful, but it is fragile and we should not idolize it. Educated Christians know that giving oneself to one's spouse is not just about carnal passion or desire, but about spiritual communion. It is about having pleasure and experiencing the tenderness of God.

A couple must cultivate healthy attitudes, openly and honestly discussing personal desires. Misconceptions of sex and a desire for secrecy could prevent you from talking about something so intimate, but this type of discussion aids the expression of personal longings and deepens sexual intimacy. Do you want your relationship to grow and mature with each other and with God? Hopefully, you will be comfortable enough with each other to communicate your desires so your sexual union will be a profound experience—a celebration of love and a fountain of life.

Our Christian Marriage

Why Marry in the Church?

Josh and Amy have been engaged for several months. They have some questions about a traditional wedding. Both come from Christian families, but their contacts with a parish are few and far between. Josh prefers a simple ceremony at town hall; a marriage in the Church does not appeal to him. Amy wants to be married in a Church so that God will bless their union. Josh is not convinced that a Christian ceremony will make any difference. He sees a number of divorces among their families and friends who were married in the Church and wants to know if things will be different with their relationship.

Do you think it makes any difference if a couple is married in a Church and seeks God's blessing?

Getting married in Church is neither complicated nor costly. The Church is solely interested in the couple's happiness and wants this happiness to be lasting. Although no one can predict the future, what is certain is that statistically speaking "trial marriages"—a contradiction in itself—fail much more frequently than traditional marriages. In fact, the essence of marriage is an unconditional commitment for life. Such a radical decision requires serious courtship, which includes growing in faith and being an active member of the Church. The whole process of marriage preparation should give the couple sufficient amount of time to get to know each other well.

First, we turn our attention to the human process. Things done halfheartedly will not last long. That is why the decision to marry should not be rushed. Marriage requires a maturity that normally comes with age, experience, and preparation. The latter takes time and involves discernment and prayer. For this reason, the Church is at the service of the couple who are also members of the community of faith.

Second, marriage responds to the most profound desires of the human heart; it's not merely a ceremony. Many cultures, including non-Christian, associate marriage with God and celebrate marriage within the context of a community and a ritual. In the Christian tradition, marriage celebrates a saving story: God is present in the community and rituals. A civil marriage is based on a written contract;

a marriage within the Church is a covenant with God. For this reason, we look at the wedding ceremony not as an end but as the beginning of a most challenging adventure—a lifelong commitment to love.

The Five Facets of the Mystery

A Russian theologian, Paul Evdokimov, once described the symbolism of wedding rings and the mystery they touch in the sacrament of matrimony. "The two rings are placed in the heart of the sanctuary, on the altar table; thus they are touching the mystery of the kingdom and, as symbols of a new destiny, they indicate the dimension into which the sacrament will lead the couple."

Others have said the rings not only *touch* the mystery, they *represent* the mystery. Like a precious stone with many facets, a marriage has many facets that will take a lifetime to discover.

The sacrament of matrimony has traditionally expressed the couple's mutual consent and "the marital act." But this is only one aspect (or facet) of marriage life. When we describe marriage as a mystery rather than sacrament, we express *all* facets of marital living, including those that precede and go beyond the celebration of the wedding ritual. In fact, the word *mystery* is meant to encompass the daily reality of marriage and family life. These facets are the essential lifeblood of harmony and happiness for any married couple. The five facets to marital life are: vocation, communion, covenant, sacrament, and family.

Vocation. *Vocation* is the door of the sacramental mystery. It means a "calling" from God to follow a divine path of holiness. From the moment a couple meets, they are already preparing for the special vocation of married life. We spend years preparing for a career, why not for the important profession of marriage? The road to excellence in all professions requires sacrifice, and sacrifice leads to maturity and growth.

Living together as a married couple involves sharing everything: ideals, resources, sufferings, and joys. Each partner continues to develop the emotional and spiritual traits of his or her personality. It is important not to try to change your spouse; rather, try to connect with your partner as he or she is. God has a marvelous plan for your family. God will bless you with his grace and he will always be with you as you fulfill this plan as husband and wife.

DYNAMIC GRAPHICS

Communion. *Communion* is the heart of marriage, a graced bond springing forth from the fountain of divine love. It flourishes in mutual self-giving, in which intimate togetherness is balanced with the need for individual space. The essential elements of this communion are love, intimacy, and sexuality. Successful couples manage the conflicts of the intimate intermingling of their lives. They adjust to each other and grow together in a healthy way. They learn to live joyfully and sacrificially with patience, prayer, faith, and God's grace.

Intimate living is a fountain of joy for couples who show tenderness, compassion, and trust for each other in the small details of ordinary life. For example, emptying the dishwasher for your spouse might be more meaningful than a fancy dinner at a restaurant. A good sense of humor and loving gestures like complimenting your spouse, writing a love note, and simply saying "I love you" are all simple actions that can renew and deepen your marriage bond. Love is not about the extraordinary, but the ordinary done in an extraordinary way.

The passion of sexual love does not guarantee success and stability in marriage. It is only when you sacrifice for your spouse that you can say in truth: "I love you." Sexual intimacy is a gift from God that grows in an atmosphere of respect within an emotionally healthy relationship.

Covenant. A *covenant* is the pledge of one person to another in marriage; it is sworn to God and seals the sacramental mystery. Christian spouses are called to see Christ's gaze in each other. Saint Paul also referred to marriage as a mirror of the love between Christ and the Church (Ephesians 5:32). The biblical covenant reveals keys we can use in daily communication: dialogue, communion, presence, and power.

Dialogue is truthful and respectful communication. This implies transparency and honesty, being an empathetic listener and a forthcoming talker, and addressing touchy matters at the appropriate time. *Communion* is lovingly sharing one's whole being in all aspects of married life. It is not coincidence that communion and communication come from the same root. *Presence* is dedicating yourself to your spouse and being available to the family. *Power* is not control; it is promoting what is good in the relationship while accepting married life for what it is. This includes mutual forgiveness, a pillar of marital stability. As Saint Paul writes in his letter to the Ephesians, "do not let the sun go down on your anger" (4:26). In sum, couples should strive for good communication and positive ways of expressing emotions.

Be aware that challenges are a part of life; there is no "quick fix" for most issues. For example, women and men may have different ways of expressing and experiencing love, of responding to one another sexually, and of communicating emotional needs. They also have different ways of expressing their points of view. Couples need to understand and accept their differences and resolve conflicts with mutual respect. Communication skills and positive conflict-solving skills can be learned. Attentive listening invigorates relationships, but continuous tensions and arrogant attitudes erode them. Unloving behavior can lead to a situation of spiritual and psychological divorce.

INDEXOPEN

Sacrament. The *sacrament* of marriage is not just the wedding ritual but the entire life of the couple. Their married love reflects God's divine love. For this reason, Christian wisdom emphasizes that the final purpose of marriage is the mutual salvation of the couple. Marriage is also a commitment rooted in our baptism, celebrated within the body of Christ, the Church, and sealed by the Eucharist. During the wedding rite, the couple offer themselves to God in communion that is life-giving and everlasting. By the grace of God, husband and wife are a sacrament to each other and a sacrament to the world.

When a couple is struggling in their relationship, they can draw strength from their sacramental oath: the public commitment that was made in the presence of God and blessed by God. They can turn to prayer and trust that God will help them forgive one another and stay together for the sake of their children.

Family. The Christian family represents the social dimension of the sacrament of marriage. When commitment to family is grounded by mature spirituality, even failures and sins can become touchstones for renewal and strength; faith saves marriages. Joint prayer and participation in the Eucharist are at the heart of married spirituality; a personal relationship with Christ is the foundation.

The first three to five years of marriage are decisive. Hard times can arrive in unforeseeable ways. When the first child arrives, the couple has to readjust their lifestyle, which can be quite challenging. The family's primary responsibility is to raise children who experience love at home so they will be able to love in turn. In this regard, the family is the perfect and first school of love. Hence, the family must be defended against the ever-increasing challenges of our secularized society. Parents must trust that God will help them get through even the toughest times. Their special mission is to be heralds of the faith with regard to their children and heralds of the Gospel in the world. With the Holy Family of Nazareth as their model, they are called to be a living sacrament of healing and compassion, forgiveness and prayer.

These five facets represent the sacramental mystery of marriage according to the Catholic tradition. We believe that the marital covenant, which is the work of God, was renewed by the love of Christ on the cross. For this reason, we call the marital covenant a sacramental mystery.

Twelve Questions Couples Ask

1 Do we have to get married through the civil court before getting married by the Church?

No, a Church wedding is civilly and ecclesiastically valid in the United States. An engaged couple does need to apply for a marriage license in the town where the marriage will take place. The couple should give the officiating priest or deacon the marriage license at the wedding rehearsal. After officiating the wedding, the priest will sign in and send it back to the appropriate office.

2 How long must the engaged couple wait before they get married?

Many dioceses require a minimum of six to nine months from the time of the couple's first visit to the priest until the date of their wedding. Once you are engaged, contact a parish priest to set a date for your marriage on the parish calendar. Because each couple and parish have different circumstances, it is critical to contact a parish priest before you set your wedding date. Dioceses require engaged couples to obtain their sacramental papers, especially their baptismal certificate, and attend a marriage-preparation workshop on the basic aspects of marital life. Your priest will explain specific requirements further.

3 How much does a Catholic wedding cost?

Many parishes ask the couple to contribute a nominal fee to the parish. The amount varies according to the policies of different dioceses and the couple's economic situation.

4 Is it better to live together before marriage as a way of getting to know each other?

No. Living together before marriage is a sin. Sexual union belongs exclusively within marriage: a life commitment of complete, definite, and faithful giving of self between a man and a woman. A relatively lengthy and chaste engagement is the best path for a couple to get to know each other and make a decision that is free and thoughtful.

5 Does the Catholic Church allow sacramental marriage between a Catholic and someone who practices another faith?

Yes. The priest or deacon must ask the bishop for special permission, but it is typically granted. It is very important that you and your partner discuss your respective faith

traditions and your plans for the religious education of your children. The Catholic partner must promise to continue observing the Catholic faith and to do his or her best to baptize any future children and raise them in the Catholic faith. This promise is made in the presence of the non-Catholic partner, who does not have to make this promise but is expected to be supportive.

6 I am pregnant. Can I still have a Church wedding?

Yes, you can. Nevertheless, it would be an error for a couple to marry only because a baby is on the way. External circumstances cannot impose life commitments. Couples should marry because they feel God's call to form a family. They should do so in freedom, and only if a mature commitment exists between them. To prevent a precipitous decision, your pastor may recommend that you wait until the baby is born before getting married. You need time and preparation to fully understand marital obligations.

7 My fiancé was previously married. Can we get married in the Church? What is an annulment?

If a previous spouse has died, you are free to marry again. In cases of civil divorce, a couple can get married in the Church as long as the prior marriage receives a decree of nullity. Sacramental marriage is a permanent commitment that cannot be dissolved. However, the Church can declare a marriage null if something essential that makes Christian marriage valid was missing from the previous marriage and, therefore, a sacramental marriage did not take place.

INDEXOPEN

8 Should I marry someone not from my own culture and way of life?

We live in a culturally diverse country. It is essential to appreciate other cultures and take advantage of the best American culture has to offer without compromising our individual spiritual identity and by preserving the best traits of our cultural heritage. Being open to cultural diversity can enrich our lives tremendously, provided we interweave both cultures in a respectful way. Each couple establishes their own way of relating to one another and their own lifestyle. Our Christian vision affirms the equality of human rights and the inherent human dignity of both husband and wife.

9 Is it possible to have a simple marriage ceremony without a Mass or many guests?

It is up to the couple. A marriage ritual without the Mass has the same validity as a marriage celebrated with the Mass. The marriage ceremony consists of an entrance procession, prayers, two Bible readings, the actual marriage ritual with the exchange of vows, the solemn blessing of the couple, and a conclusion. Share your wishes and concerns with your priest or deacon.

10 Do we have to participate in the sacrament of reconciliation before getting married?

Yes, you should embrace this sacrament as an encounter of grace, healing, and freedom with a forgiving and compassionate God through the liberating love of Jesus Christ. Supporting the need of spiritual rebirth and renewal at this decisive stage of your lives, this sacrament is a grace-filled and profoundly joyful experience.

11 If "unsolvable" problems arise in our marriage, to whom should we turn?

You should first attempt to resolve any problems on your own. If the conflict does not originate from a serious problem such as addiction or abuse, it often stems from a communication problem. Only you can resolve your hurt emotions and misunderstandings. This is a good beginning: examine your own motives, try to give up arrogant attitudes, begin talking and listening attentively to your spouse. Don't blame each other or pretend one of you is always right.

Seek assistance from a third party such as your priest or a marital counselor—particularly if you are unable to speak to one another or if you have frequent conflicts and fears—*before* the relationship ends in spiritual separation. It can be a mistake to bring problems to your parents or family; they may not see things objectively or may feel the need to take sides. Ignoring your conflicts is a big mistake that can lead to a variety of problems, including abandoning your family or engaging in an illicit relationship.

12 How can we enrich our marriage as our family grows?

Just as a beautiful garden has weeds and needs cultivation, a marriage needs loving and tender care throughout your lives. Your relationship will continue to grow through meaningful conversations and shared interests, frustrations, and aspirations. A healthy couple reserves time to relax by themselves *and* with their children. A united couple must protect their marriage against the assault of secular values and a culture of death. Maintain close relationships with other couples who share your faith ideals. Participate in the celebration of Mass together, be active in parish life (sacraments of initiation, religious education, and so on), and pray together as a family. Participating in spiritual exercises and retreats, such as marriage encounters, can be an excellent way of strengthening and rejuvenating your family hopes and expectations.

INDEXOPEN

Our Wedding

PAMELA HUMMELSHEIM

John and Karina are engaged. Their families and friends offer them advice on marriage. Karina's mother noted the first couple of years can be full of ups and downs, but good marriages get through them with communication, flexibility, and love. Their priest, Father Taylor, said sacrificial love, unbreakable respect, responsible commitment, and living faith are like the couple's hands on the paddles of a little boat, carrying it forward. These four hands can happily navigate the river of married life.

What is the best advice you've been given about marriage?

In our individualistic society, courting dramatically differs from one couple to another. Nevertheless, some Christian families preserve marriage traditions and rites of passage to give couples support. These rites are part of a transitional process and time of preparation for the shift from single to married life.

These traditions are divided into two phases: the engagement, which can be formal or informal and includes a marriage commitment, and the wedding itself. Some parishes traditionally introduce engaged couples at the end of Mass, for example. The presiding priest invites the couples to come to the sanctuary. After reciting a prayer, the priest invites the assembly to extend their hands with him for the blessing. The assembly's congratulating applause concludes this "rite."

The saying "no man is an island" applies to engaged couples as well. Interaction with family and community support can enhance the couple's time of preparation and prevent a feeling of isolation. However, be aware that preparing for a wedding takes a lot of energy and time and can bring up some family-of-origin issues. Couples should always present a united front when these issues arise.

The wedding is often held at the bride's parish. The time dedicated to planning your wedding will be substantial and can conflict with the commitments of work and other daily obligations. By taking time to plan the details well in advance, you will be free to fully enjoy the most special day of your lives. Your wedding day is an encounter with God and a memorable feast of love and joy with your family members and close friends.

The Wedding Ritual: A Great Celebration of Life and Love

You, as a couple, should not be satisfied with a mere ceremony. Your wedding should be a living celebration filled with joy and a spiritual atmosphere. Take time to prepare and enjoy it. The bride and groom are the ministers of the sacramental wedding. The priest or deacon is the witness, presiding at the wedding and responsible for the ritual.

The wedding ritual is usually celebrated during the Mass. Traditionally, it begins with the solemn procession of the wedding party. When they arrive at the altar, the father or some other male family member hands the bride to the groom, who is accompanied by the best man. The symbolism is apparent: The support of family brings you to the altar. The couple also relies on the sup-

COMSTOCK

Preparations for the Wedding

- *Meet with your priest or deacon, who will give you the instructions for your wedding and marriage preparation.*
- *Have your baptism certificates ready. These can be obtained from the parish where you were baptized and must be issued no more than six months before the wedding.*
- *Attend a marriage preparation program (also known as pre-Cana). The class is usually completed with other married couples, and a priest or deacon is usually present to address the sacramental and spiritual dimensions of marriage. In some dioceses this preparation is completed in two days (for example, a weekend retreat). Other dioceses might offer a series of evening classes over one month or more.*
- *Choose a wedding date and register it on the parish calendar.*
- *Have a formal interview with the priest or deacon, who will fill out the official marriage register of the parish. At this interview, he will speak of the sacramental significance of marriage and the importance of spiritual preparation for your wedding, including taking part in the sacrament of reconciliation.*
- *Make preparations for the wedding ceremony, such as the planning of the liturgy, music, and flowers. Your priest or deacon will give you insights and suggestions, but you can share your personal preferences for the wedding celebration with him, such as traditions of your cultural background. Current liturgical rituals are somewhat flexible and encourage joyful and prayerful participation of all the people involved.*
- *Obtain a marriage license from the city where the wedding will take place; check your state's requirements to be sure the license doesn't expire before your wedding date.*
- *The wedding rehearsal usually takes place a day or two before the wedding. The main participants, such as parents and the wedding party, should be present as well as anyone participating in the entrance procession*

CORBIS

port of friends, who are represented by bridesmaids and groomsmen, beyond the ceremony itself.

The marriage ritual begins immediately after the scriptural readings and the homily as follows:

- *Introductory address by the celebrant*
- *Statement of intentions*
- *Consent, or exchange of marriage vows.*

Consent is the heart of the marriage ritual. Turning to each other, joining hands, and romantically gazing into one another's eyes, the couple professes their marriage vows.

The following is the traditional formula:

The groom says,

I, N., take you, N., to be my wife. I promise to be true to you in good times and in bad, in sickness and in health. I will love you and honor you all the days of my life.

The bride says,

I, N., take you, N., to be my husband. I promise to be true to you in good times and in bad, in sickness and in health. I will love you and honor you all the days of my life.

The rings are blessed and exchanged. The groom places his wife's ring on her finger, saying,

N., take this ring as a sign of my love and fidelity. In the name of the Father, and of the Son, and of the Holy Spirit.

The bride places her husband's ring on his finger, saying,

N., take this ring as a sign of my love and fidelity. In the name of the Father, of the Son, and of the Holy Spirit.

The bride, groom, celebrants, and assembly pray the Our Father. The nuptial blessing follows. As the couple kneels together, the priest prays over them. After this, the peace of Christ is exchanged.

In some parishes, the lighting of the marriage candle follows. The couple lights two little candles on the altar. Immediately after professing their vows, they will use these candles to light their marriage candle together, symbolizing their covenant.

In some parishes, the newly married couple will go to Our Lady's altar before the recessional hymn. The couple may be accompanied by their godparents. The bride places a bouquet of flowers on the altar and entrusts her marriage and future family to Mary.

The final blessing concludes the wedding celebration. After the priest's blessing, the newly wed spouses exit. The other participants follow them at a short distance.

The Only Predictors of Marital Happiness You Need

You want your love to last forever, but it's hard to predict the future. Rather than worrying about the unknown, focus on the things you do know. Marriage should be undertaken only by a person capable of growth on several levels: physical and spiritual, affective and sexual, personal and social, natural and supernatural. The five pillars of successful dating and the five facets of marriage integrate those dimensions and empower you to grow in each of them. They are reliable predictors of later marital stability and happiness.

Marriage is earthly and human but, with God's grace, it reaches beyond itself to a sacramental mystery. The many-splendored reality of love, good personal traits and behaviors, similarity of values, and healthy individual skills are basic elements of a successful partnership. However, those human values rest on a spiritual foundation: God's abiding presence in your home.

Happiness is a state of mind that lies within each of us. You should love yourself and never allow resentment or lack of respect to erode the emotional attachment of your heart and your beautiful, holy bond of marriage. Therefore, do not put unfair and unrealistic expectations on each other. Marriage is your vocation and a calling from God, the third person guaranteeing your sacramental bond.

INDEXOPEN